Science Biographies

Alexander Graham
Bell

Catherine Chambers

Raintree
Chicago, Illinois

Edited by Dan Nunn, Adam Miller, and Diyan Leake
Designed by Cynthia Akiyoshi
Picture research by Tracy Cummins
Production by Helen McCreath
Originated by Capstone Global Library
Printed and bound in China

17 16 15 14 13
10 9 8 7 6 5 4 3 2 1

Library of Congress Cataloging-in-Publication Data
Chambers, Catherine, 1954- author.
  Alexander Graham Bell / Catherine Chambers.
    pages cm.—(Science biographies)
  Summary: "This book traces the life of Alexander Graham
Bell, from his early childhood and education through his
sources of inspiration and challenges faced, early successes,
and the invention for which he is best known: the telephone. A
timeline at the end of the book summarizes key milestones and
achievements of Bell's life."—Provided by publisher.
  Includes bibliographical references and index.
  ISBN 978-1-4109-6238-6 (hb)—ISBN 978-1-4109-6245-4 (pb)
  1. Bell, Alexander Graham, 1847-1922—Juvenile literature. 2.
Inventors—United States—Biography—Juvenile literature. 3.
Telephone—History—Juvenile literature. I. Title.
  TK6143.B4C44 2014
  621.385092—dc23   2013014219

Acknowledgments
We would like to thank the following for permission to
reproduce photographs: Alamy pp. 20 (© Historical Art
Collection (HAC)), 24 (© bilwissedition Ltd. & Co. KG); The
Bridgeman Art Library p. 22 (Science Museum, London, UK);
Corbis pp. 8 (© Dr. Gilbert H. Grosvenor/National Geographic
Society), 17 (© Bettmann); Getty Images pp. 5 (Petrified
Collection), 9 (Science & Society Picture Library), 10 (Dr.
Gilbert H. Grosvenor), 13 (Vintage Images), 15 (Keystone-
France/Gamma-Keystone via Getty Images), 18 (Library of
Congress - edited version © Science Faction), 19 (SSPL), 21
(Leemage), 26 (Ira Block/National Geographic); Library of
Congress Prints and Photographs Division pp. 4, 6, 11, 14,
16, 25, design elements; National Archives design elements;
National Geographic Stock pp. 7 (Bell Family), 12 (Dr. Gilbert
H. Grosvenor), 27 (Bell Collection); Photo Researchers p. 28
(Science Source); Shutterstock design elements (© Zigzag
Mountain Art, © Morphart Creation, © Rambleon,
© PhotoHouse, © Hans Kwaspen, © stockpackshot);
Wikipedia p. 23 (AgnosticPreachersKid).

Cover photographs reproduced with permission of
SuperStock (Science Faction) and Library of Congress,
Manuscript Division.

Every effort has been made to contact copyright holders of
material reproduced in this book. Any omissions will
be rectified in subsequent printings if notice is given to
the publisher.

All the Internet addresses (URLs) given in this book were valid
at the time of going to press. However, due to the dynamic
nature of the Internet, some addresses may have changed, or
sites may have changed or ceased to exist since publication.
While the author and publisher regret any inconvenience this
may cause readers, no responsibility for any such changes can
be accepted by either the author or the publisher.

Contents

Some words are shown in **bold**, like this. You can find out what they mean by looking in the glossary.

Who Was Alexander Graham Bell?

Imagine a world without instant communication. No computers, no cell phones—or any kind of telephone! This was life over 150 years ago.

Into this world was born a remarkable man. He was fascinated by sound and how it travels. His name was Alexander Bell, and he was born on March 3, 1847, in Edinburgh, Scotland. Bell became a famous teacher of speech, especially for the deaf. But no one could have guessed that he would invent the telephone and change the world. When he was a boy, everyone called him Aleck, so we will, too.

Bell became a highly respected teacher and scientist as well as an inventor.

MESSAGES ACROSS THE WORLD

Sending letters by horse, carriage, or even pigeon was a slow way of communicating. So, too, were smoke signals, flags, and drumbeats. This traditional world of communication was transformed by **telegraphy**, which was invented just before Aleck was born.

Top technology in the 1840s

Telegraph messages were sent in **code** along electrical pulses through wires. At the receiving end, these changed into a code that could be read on a telegraphy machine. The first working system was demonstrated by the American inventors F. B. Morse and Alfred Vail in 1837.

A Passion for Sound

Aleck came from a family that was obsessed with sound, especially the human voice. Both his father and grandfather taught **elocution**. Elocution lessons help people to speak clearly.

PERSONAL PASSIONS

Aleck's mother was Eliza Grace Symonds. Eliza was deaf, but she taught her three sons with the help of finger signs. Aleck spoke to her by pressing his lips on her forehead so she could feel the vibrations of the words.

Aleck's father, Alexander Melville Bell, was a professor of speech therapy at Edinburgh University. Young Aleck was inspired by his family's love of communication and experiments.

Alexander Melville Bell (1819–1905), shown here, was the son of yet another speech expert, Alexander Bell (1790–1865).

Even Aleck's pet dog, Trouve, could not escape his interest. He moved Trouve's voice box and lips with his fingers to make noises that sounded a little like words!

Aleck is on the far left, posing with his family. His brothers are Melville (Melly) and Edward (Ted).

The sound of silence

The science of speech therapy for the deaf was still new when Aleck was a boy.

Sign languages had been used in different cultures for hundreds of years. Interest in how the mouth and voice box produce words only grew after James Rush published a book about it in 1827.

Learning Alone

When Aleck was 11, he met an exciting family friend named Graham. Aleck decided to add "Graham" to his own name.

One thing that Aleck was not interested in was going to school! As young children, the three Bell brothers were taught by their mother. Then, at age 11, Aleck was sent to the Royal Edinburgh High School. He hated it and left when he was 15.

When Aleck went to the Royal Edinburgh High School, it was in this serious-looking building.

Aleck's parents sent him to London, England. Here, his grandfather educated him in an exciting, interesting way. In addition to normal classes, Aleck learned to play the piano. This gave him many sounds to study!

Staying in tune

Aleck's piano playing led him to experiment with **tuning forks**. These are used to measure the musical notes of instruments to see if they are still in tune. But Aleck used them to measure **tones** of spoken words—how the sound goes up and down. This later helped him as a teacher of speech and in his quest to develop the telephone.

The long **prongs** of tuning forks vary in length. When they are struck, their vibrations make the sound of different notes. They are made of metal that is not too stiff to wobble.

A Young Expert

At just 16 years old, Aleck became a teacher of music and elocution at Weston House Academy in Elgin, Scotland. Aleck liked his students to have fun! At the school, Aleck was able to take free classes in advanced Greek and Latin.

[ENGLISH ALPHABET OF VISIBLE SPEECH, Expressed in the Names of Numbers and Objects.]

The Visible Speech chart has diagrams and symbols to show how to mouth and sound words.

A FAMILY AFFAIR

Professor Bell invented a teaching tool for the deaf called **Visible Speech**. His sons showed a great interest in it. The tool was a chart showing how the mouth shapes each sound as it is spoken.

Professor Bell took this picture of Aleck as a teenager in Edinburgh.

Sounding it out

Try saying the simple word *yes*, very slowly. You will notice that the sound starts at the back of your mouth and ends at the front. The tongue changes place. Your mouth moves its shape. *Yes* really isn't a simple word at all!

Tragedy and Travel

In the 1860s, Bell's father and Melly traveled to Canada and the United States to meet other speech experts. Tragedy struck the family when first Ted, then Melly, died of a disease called **tuberculosis**.

In 1870, Bell and his parents moved to Canada to breathe healthier air. Bell saw job opportunities over the border in the United States and was soon working in a new school for the deaf. He had huge success as a **speech therapist** and was made professor of vocal physiology at Boston University in 1873.

This is the school where Bell (top row, far right) transformed speech therapy.

TAKING UP A CHALLENGE

Across the United States, scientists were working on new telegraph systems. They were trying to come up with a telegraph design that was reliable and that could transport more than just a single message at a time. Bell took up the challenge.

Telegraph messaging was often frustrating. The lines often broke or were jammed.

No time to sleep

At night, Bell secretly worked on a multiple telegraph system. His parents thought it was an unnecessary distraction from teaching. Bell's ideas came from the sound vibrations of his tuning fork experiments. He called his project the **harmonic telegraph**.

Lucky Breaks

Bell lived in the home of Thomas Sanders, a wealthy man and the father of one of his students, five-year-old George. George was born deaf and could not communicate. Bell's skills transformed this little boy's life, and his father was very grateful.

Sanders took a special interest in Bell's research. He knew that multiple telegraph messages could lead to a pot of gold! By 1874, Bell had a second investor. He was Gardiner Hubbard, the father of another deaf student, Mabel.

Gardiner Hubbard was a lawyer but was interested in supplying water, gas, and communications to the public.

A FAMOUS ADDRESS

Another interested supporter was Moses Farmer, who found rooms where Bell could conduct his experiments. These were five floors above an electrical store owned by a man named Charles Williams. The building was at 109 Court Street in Boston. This soon became a very famous address.

An electric miracle

Bell needed electricity for his research. There was no regular supply of it in the early 1870s, so he had to use batteries. He had to conduct his experiments under dim gaslight. Long-lasting light bulbs were invented by Thomas Edison only in 1879.

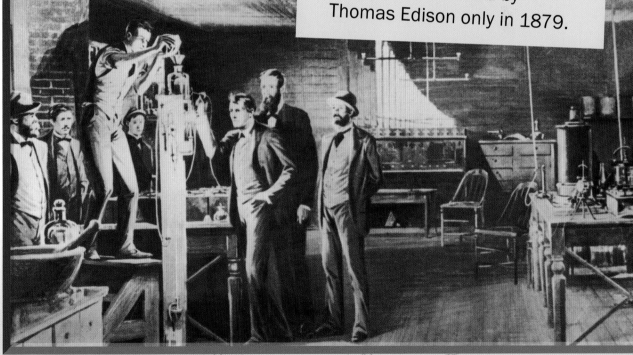

A Perfect Partner

Bell was working far too hard and needed an assistant. Moses Farmer suggested young Tom Watson, who worked in Charles Williams's electrical store below. Watson had made a lot of telegraphic equipment and was an excellent **machinist**. Perfect!

Thomas Augustus Watson was a bookkeeper and carpenter before he became a machinist.

CHASING HIS DREAM

Bell and Watson worked hard on the telegraph. They developed the telephone in their spare time. On the hot night of June 2, 1875, Watson twanged one of the metal connections, which they called **reeds**. The reed vibrated like Bell's tuning forks had, creating different tones. Bell realized that he could transmit many sounds at once, along a single wire.

The telegraph race

In Chicago, another inventor, Elisha Gray (pictured here), was perfecting his telegraph machine—and a telephone! Bell said, "It is a neck and neck race between Mr. Gray and myself... He has the advantage over me in being a practical electrician, but I have reason to believe that I am better acquainted with the phenomenon of sound than he is."

The Magic Moment

On March 10, 1876, Bell and Watson were in their attic trying to set up a telephone link. Bell was in one room and Watson was in the room next to it. The telephone apparatus was all set up. They had so far achieved just a few muffled sounds, nothing more.

Eureka!

Watson was very surprised when he suddenly heard Bell calling him loudly through the receiver. Watson recalled later that Bell had accidentally spilled acid on his pants. Acid burns! So Bell yelled out to Watson, whose telephone picked up the message, loud and clear!

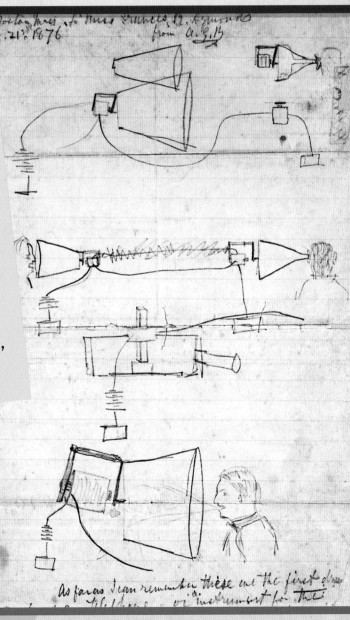

These are Bell's original notes and diagram of that amazing first phone call. The papers later became very important in proving that Bell had invented the first working telephone.

No time to sleep

Bell's first telephone was a **liquid transmitter**, like this one. The liquids were water and acid, which carried the electronic signals. After that first incredible phone call, Bell redesigned his invention. His new telephone used an **electromagnet** to carry the signals, not liquid.

Triumph for the Telephone!

Bell needed to make people aware of his new invention. Mabel Hubbard encouraged him to take it to the Philadelphia Centennial Exposition. Bell demonstrated his telephone on June 25, 1876, and it was an overnight sensation.

The Centennial Exposition was a celebration of 100 years of American cultural and industrial progress.

Protecting his telephone

Earlier that year, Gardiner Hubbard had submitted Bell's harmonic telegraph to the U.S. **Patent** Office. A patent protects ideas from being copied.

In the patent papers, Bell had included an explanation and sketch of his telephone as well as telegraph. This meant that his telegraph patent also protected his telephone invention. Bell's patent number—174,465—is one of the most famous in the world.

Soon, everyone wanted to make phone calls! Telephone exchanges linked up callers through a switchboard that connected telephone lines.

Bitter rivals

From 1876 until 1901, other scientists battled in courts of law to claim the telephone invention. There were the Americans Elisha Gray and Thomas Edison. There were also the Italian Antonio Meucci, the Frenchman Charles Borseul, the German Johann Philipp Reis—and others! But Bell won in the end.

Remembering Friends

In 1877, Bell set up the Bell Telephone Company with his loyal supporters, Watson, Hubbard, and Sanders. They rented out telephones to the public—the beginning of a global industry. The company later became the American Telephone and Telegraph Company (AT&T), which is successful to this day.

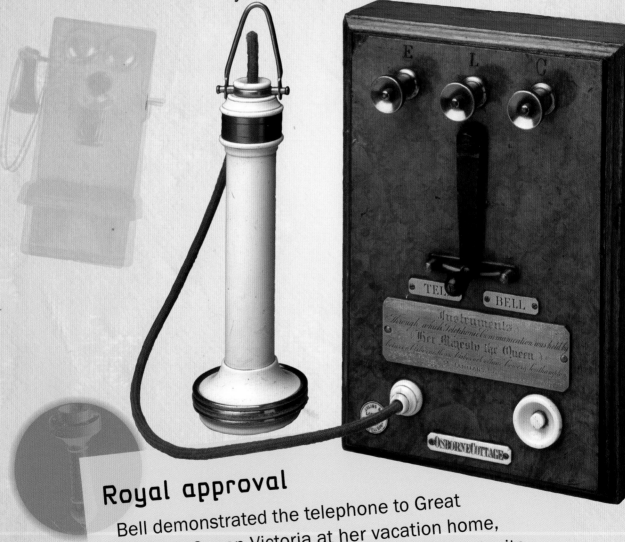

Royal approval

Bell demonstrated the telephone to Great Britain's Queen Victoria at her vacation home, Osborne House. She thought the invention "quite extraordinary" and later purchased this elegant phone for Osborne House.

PERSONAL HAPPINESS

Also in 1877, Bell married Mabel Hubbard. After the wedding, they went on a year-long trip abroad. Of course, the telephone came with them, and their honeymoon became a grand promotional tour. Mabel told Bell she preferred his first name spelled Alec. So, he changed it. That's love for you!

PRIZES AND PASSIONS

In 1880, Bell won the Prix Volta, a prize set up in honor of Alessandro Volta, the inventor of the battery. With the 50,000 French **francs**, Bell built the Volta Laboratory and Volta Bureau in Georgetown, Washington, D.C. Here he promoted research into deafness, sound recording, and other serious science.

The Volta Laboratory is also called Alexander Graham Bell House.

Moving On

Bell's generous Volta Prize meant that he could sell his share in Bell Telephone Company. He happily returned to science and the advancement of deaf people.

A STREAM OF SCIENCE

In 1880, Bell invented the **photophone**. This transmitted words along a beam of light, not a wire, like the cell phone 100 years later! Bell also improved upon Thomas Edison's **graphophone**—a sound player and recorder.

Bell preferred his photophone invention to the telephone.

TRYING TO SAVE THE PRESIDENT

U.S. President James Garfield was shot by Charles Guiteau on July 2, 1881. No one could find the bullet in his body, although Bell tried to locate it with a magnetic device he had developed. On September 19, Garfield died, but Bell's invention later saved lives in the Boer War (1899–1902) and World War I (1914–1918).

Bell and Mabel had two daughters: Elise (born 1878) and Marian (born 1880).

A teacher for Helen Keller

Helen Keller (1880–1968) was a famous writer, lecturer, and political activist. She was also totally deaf and blind. Bell helped find an amazing teacher for her, Anne Sullivan. Helen became Bell and Mabel's lifelong friend.

The Science of Nature

Bell wanted his family to remember wonderful vacations. So, in 1885, he bought a summerhouse on the island of Cape Breton, in northern Canada. The island lies off Nova Scotia, which means "New Scotland." Its wild landscapes reminded Bell of Scotland, although he became a proud American.

Bell and Mabel loved the scenery at their house on Cape Breton.

Working vacations

Bell could not stop working, even on vacation! He built a laboratory at his summerhouse. While he worked, he took an interest in the nature and landscapes around him.

In 1888, Bell helped Mabel's father set up the National Geographic Society, which encouraged interest in travel, exploration, and science. He did a lot of work for its famous publication, the *National Geographic*, and another called *Science*. *National Geographic* inspires people to this day.

Flying high

Bell spent many hours studying birds and how they flew. From this, he designed a kite built from **tetrahedrons**, which are three-sided pyramid shapes. The shape was so strong that it was later used to construct buildings. Bell designed a plane and a **hydrofoil**, which is a boat that runs on skis.

Remembering Bell

Bell continued working until he died on August 2, 1922, at age 75, with Mabel at his side. Across the United States, the phones stopped ringing for a minute as a mark of respect.

Bell is remembered as a famous scientist. More than this, he wanted to do good, especially for people who could not hear the voices around them. He was always loyal to the people who helped him and grateful to the parents who nurtured him.

Bell is still remembered as one of the world's most famous scientists and inventors.

What's next for the telephone?

Today, there are designs for cell phones strapped around the wrist. Others will eventually show 3D images or be powered by the Sun's energy. Bell probably would not be surprised!

Timeline

1847 Alexander Bell is born in Scotland on March 3

1858 Attends Royal Edinburgh High School

1862 Travels to London and stays with his grandfather for a year

1863 Teaches music and elocution in Scotland

1864 Bell's father develops Visible Speech, to help deaf people to communicate

1867 Bell's brother Ted dies

1870 Bell's brother Melly dies. The Bells move to Canada.

1873 Bell teaches Visible Speech and becomes a professor at Boston University; joins the race to develop a multiple-message telegraph

1874 Teaches two deaf children. Their fathers, Thomas Sanders and Gardiner Hubbard, finance Bell's research.

1875 Tom Watson becomes Bell's assistant

1876 Bell receives a U.S. patent for his telegraph and telephone designs on March 7; makes the first telephone call to Watson on March 10; takes the phone to the Centennial World Exposition in Philadelphia

1877 Bell, Watson, Sanders, and Hubbard set up the Bell Telephone Company. Bell marries Mabel Hubbard.

1878 The Bells' first daughter, Elsie, is born in May

1880 The Bells' second daughter, Marian, is born in February. Bell wins the Volta Prize; sets up the Volta Laboratory and Volta Bureau to research deafness and other science.

1885 The Bells buy a house on Cape Breton island in northern Canada. Bell sets up a laboratory there.

1922 Alexander Graham Bell dies on August 2

Glossary

code symbols or signs that are changed into words for communicating

electromagnet magnet with a wire coil around it that generates an electric current

elocution speaking clearly

franc money used in France before 2002

graphophone machine that plays and records sound, especially music

harmonic telegraph telegraph that sends more than one message at once

hydrofoil boat that moves on ski-like stilts

liquid transmitter telephone that uses water and acid to generate an electric signal

machinist skilled worker who can make machines from a design

patent certificate that protects an idea from being copied

photophone machine that transmits messages along a light beam

prong long, thin piece of metal like that on a fork

reed strip of metal or other material that vibrates to make a note

speech therapist someone who helps people to speak clearly

telegraphy sending messages in code along wires

tetrahedron pyramid shape with three sides and a base

tone rise or fall of a sound and its quality, like a note

tuberculosis lung disease that was hard to cure until the 1950s

tuning fork metal stick with prongs that vibrate to give a note or tone

Visible Speech method of teaching deaf people to speak through diagrams of the mouth and symbols of sounds

Find Out More

Books

Berger, Gilda, and Melvin Berger. *Did You Invent the Phone Alone, Alexander Graham Bell?* (Science Supergiants). New York: Scholastic, 2007.

Kulling, Monica. *Listen Up! Alexander Graham Bell's Talking Machine* (Step into Reading). New York: Random House, 2007.

Rivera, Sheila. *Alexander Graham Bell: A Life of Helpfulness* (Pull Ahead Books). Minneapolis: Lerner, 2007.

Internet sites

Facthound offers a safe, fun way to find Internet sites related to this book. All of the sites on Facthound have been researched by our staff.

Here's all you do:
Visit **www.facthound.com**
Type in this code: 9781410962386

Places to visit

Alexander Graham Bell National Historic Site
159 Chebucto Street
Baddeck, Nova Scotia B0E 1B0
Canada
www.pc.gc.ca/lhn-nhs/ns/grahambell/index.aspx

Exploratorium
Pier 15
San Francisco, California 94111
www.exploratorium.edu

National Museum of American History
National Mall at 14th Street and Constitution Avenue, N.W.
Washington, D.C. 20001
americanhistory.si.edu

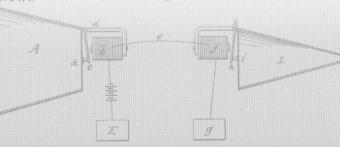

Index